Whose Hat Is This?

Whose Is It?

A Look at Hats Workers Wear— Hard, Tall, and Shiny

by Sharon Katz Cooper

illustrated by Amy Bailey Muehlenhardt

PICTURE WINDOW BOOKS
Minneapolis, Minnesota

Special thanks to our advisers for their expertise:

Rick Levine, Publisher
Made To Measure and Uniform Market News Magazine
Highland Park, Illinois

Susan Kesselring, M.A., Literacy Educator
Rosemount–Apple Valley–Eagan (Minnesota) School District

Editor: Christianne Jones
Designer: Joe Anderson
Page Production: Amy Bailey Muehlenhardt, Zach Trover
Editorial Director: Carol Jones
Creative Director: Keith Griffin
The illustrations in this book were created digitally.

Picture Window Books
1710 Roe Crest Drive
North Mankato, MN 56003
www.capstonepub.com

All books published by Picture Window Books
are manufactured with paper containing at least
10 percent post-consumer waste.

Library of Congress Cataloging-in-Publication Data
Cooper, Sharon Katz.
Whose hat is this? : a look at hats workers wear—hard, tall, and shiny / by Sharon Katz Cooper ;
illustrated by Amy Bailey Muehlenhardt.
p. cm. — (Whose is it?)
Includes bibliographical references and index.
ISBN 978-1-4048-1600-8 (hardcover)
ISBN 978-1-4048-1976-4 (paperback)
1. Hats—Juvenile literature. I. Muehlenhardt, Amy Bailey, 1974- ill. II. Title. III. Series.

GT2110.C66 2006
391.4'3—dc22   2005021849

Printed in the United States of America in North Mankato, Minnesota.
112012   006958R

Put on your thinking cap and guess whose hat is whose.

There are hard hats and soft hats, square hats and round hats. There are even very tall hats. Some workers wear hats to keep warm. Others wear hats to stay clean. A hat can block sun from a worker's eyes. A hat can protect a head from getting hurt.

Hats come in all shapes and sizes. Can you guess whose hat is whose?

Look in the back for more information about hats.

3

Whose hat is this,
so bright and shiny?

This is a firefighter's helmet.

She runs into burning
buildings to put out fires.
Her helmet keeps her
head safe from falling
objects and extreme heat.

Fun Fact: Firefighters' helmets are red, yellow, or
neon colored so they can be quickly seen from far
away or through smoke.

Whose hat is this, hanging over a face?

This is a beekeeper's hat.

A beekeeper raises bees for honey. She reaches into hives buzzing with bees to get the honey. Her hat covers her face and protects her from stings.

Fun Fact: Beekeepers also wear coveralls and long gloves to protect the rest of their bodies from bee stings.

Whose hat is this, so tall and clean?

This is a chef's hat.

His hat is also called a toque. His white hat shows that his kitchen is clean. The chef in charge of a restaurant wears the tallest hat.

Fun Fact: A chef's hat might have 100 pleats. These pleats show that a great chef can cook an egg 100 different ways.

Whose hat is this, with a polished silver badge?

This is a police officer's cap.

It is part of her uniform. A police officer's cap helps people find her quickly in a crowd because no one else will be wearing the same cap.

Fun Fact: The badges, emblems, and nameplate on the uniform are part of the insignia that a person in uniform wears. It shows what town the officer works in or what kind of skills she has.

Whose hat is this, so round and strong?

This is a football player's helmet.

When one football player tackles another one, his helmet keeps his head safe if he hits the ground or another player.

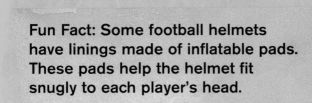

Fun Fact: Some football helmets have linings made of inflatable pads. These pads help the helmet fit snugly to each player's head.

14

Whose hat is this, shining in the night?

15

This is an astronaut's helmet.

It is part of his spacesuit. Up in space there is no air. His helmet gives him air to breathe and keeps his body at a steady temperature.

Fun Fact: It is very cold up in space, so astronauts must wear special suits with their helmets. These suits help the astronauts stay warm.

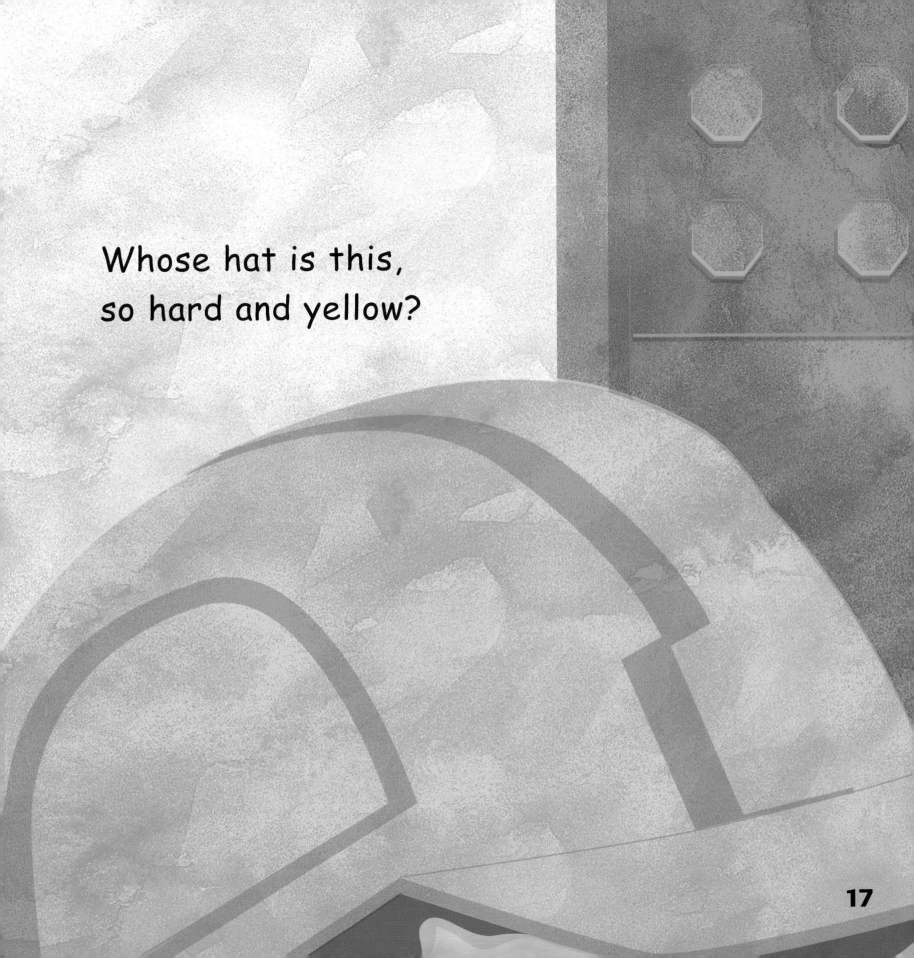

Whose hat is this,
so hard and yellow?

17

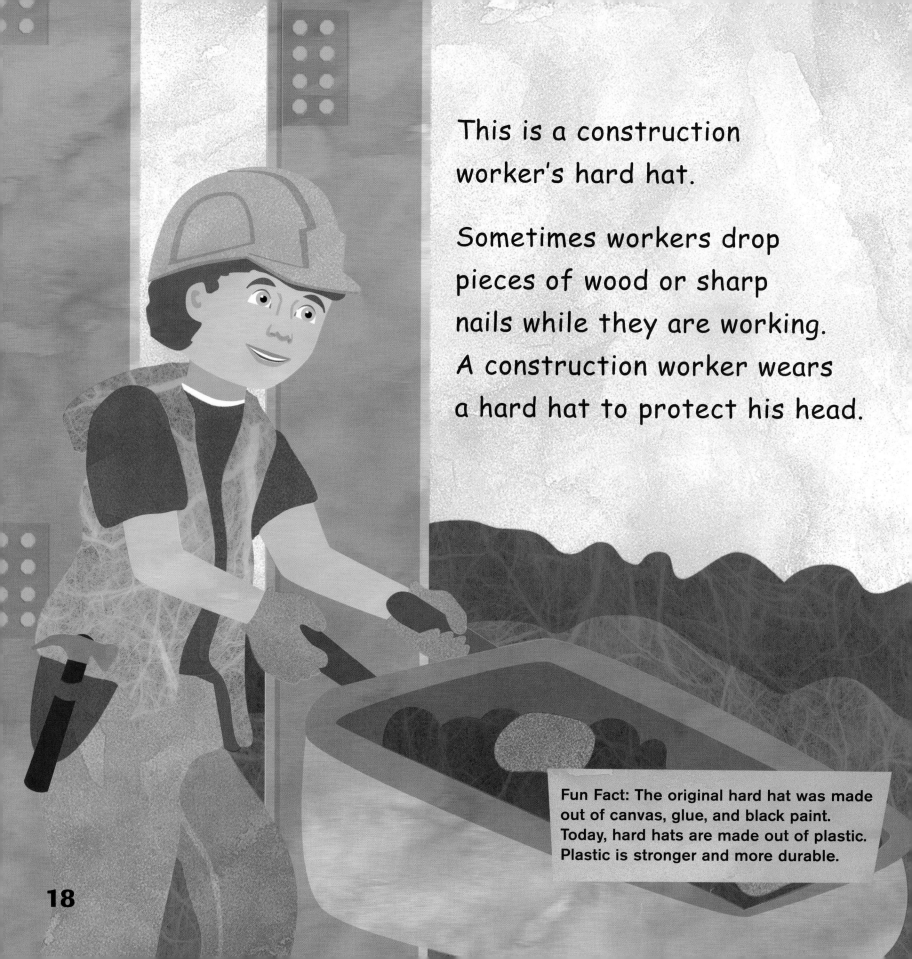

This is a construction worker's hard hat.

Sometimes workers drop pieces of wood or sharp nails while they are working. A construction worker wears a hard hat to protect his head.

Fun Fact: The original hard hat was made out of canvas, glue, and black paint. Today, hard hats are made out of plastic. Plastic is stronger and more durable.

Whose hat is this,
so warm and snug?

19

This is your hat!

When it is cold outside,
it keeps your head warm.
When it snows, it keeps
your head dry.

Fun Fact: Hats can be made from
yarn, fleece, wool, cotton, or leather.
Some winter hats even have flaps
to cover your ears.

20

Just for Fun

Point to the picture of the hat
described in each sentence.

* I have a special netting to protect a worker's face.

beekeeper's hat

* I have a shiny badge and stand out in a crowd.

police officer's cap

* I protect an athlete's head.

football player's helmet

All About Hats

Important Hats

In Egyptian, Roman, and Greek times, hats showed which people were thought of as more important than others. People who wore bigger, taller hats were more important and held a higher rank in the community.

Hat Talk

People have many sayings about hats. Have you ever heard someone say, "Hats off to you?" That means you did a good job. If a person says "keep it under your hat," it means you should keep a secret.

First Hard Hats

The first hard hat zone in the United States was at the Golden Gate Bridge construction site in San Francisco in the early 1900s.

Hat Trick

Three goals made by one player in a soccer game or hockey game is called a hat trick. This started from the British game of cricket in the 1800s. If you scored three times in a cricket game, you were often given a hat by your team.

Glossary

canvas—strong, heavy cloth

construction—to build something

coveralls—a one-piece suit you wear over your other clothes

durable—able to last a long time

inflatable—can be filled with air

insignia—badges and medals that show someone has certain skills or awards

neon—extremely bright

pleat—a special kind of fold

tackle—to knock down another person

To Learn More

More Books to Read

Corbett, Sara. *Hats Off to Hats!* Chicago:
    Children's Press, 1995.

Morris, Ann. *Hats, Hats, Hats*. New York:
    Mulberry Books, 1993.

Perl, Lila. *From Top Hats to Baseball Caps, From
    Bustles to Blue Jeans: Why We Dress the Way
    We Do*. New York: Clarion Books, 1990.

Whitty, Helen. *Hats, Gloves, and Footwear*.
    Philadelphia: Chelsea House, 2001.

On the Web

FactHound offers a safe, fun way to find Web
sites related to topics in this book. All of the sites on
FactHound have been researched by our staff.

1. Visit *www.facthound.com*
2. Type in this special code: 1404816003
3. Click on the FETCH IT button.

Your trusty FactHound will fetch the best sites for you!

Index

Look for all of the books in the Whose Is It? series:

Whose Coat Is This?
1-4048-1598-8

Whose Ears Are These?
1-4048-0004-2

Whose Eyes Are These?
1-4048-0005-0

Whose Feet Are These?
1-4048-0006-9

Whose Food Is This?
1-4048-0607-5

Whose Gloves Are These?
1-4048-1599-6

Whose Hat Is This?
1-4048-1600-3

Whose House Is This?
1-4048-0608-3

Whose Legs Are These?
1-4048-0007-7

Whose Mouth Is This?
1-4048-0008-5

Whose Nose Is This?
1-4048-0009-3

Whose Shadow Is This?
1-4048-0609-1

Whose Shoes Are These?
1-4048-1601-1

Whose Skin Is This?
1-4048-0010-7

Whose Sound Is This?
1-4048-0610-5

Whose Spots Are These?
1-4048-0611-3

Whose Tail Is This?
1-4048-0011-5

Whose Tools Are These?
1-4048-1602-X

Whose Vehicle Is This?
1-4048-1603-8

Whose Work Is This?
1-4048-0612-1